French Chic Wherever You Are

Petite lessons in French diet, staying slim, beauty, Parisian style, charm, elegance & mystique to embrace your inner Frenchness anywhere in the world

Caroline Dion

Contents

partake in le binge drinking

Introduction

Bonjour! Sometimes I find modern times just too loud, brash, inelegant and 'in-your-face' and I dream of skipping off to enchanting Paris or pretty Provence so I can sit in an adorable little French café, sip on a delicious drink and flip through a newspaper or magazine whilst I admire the chic and stylish, yet slightly 'undone', French *hommes et femmes* as they go about their day. I would pop into the local *boulangerie* for a still-warm, freshly-baked baguette or pain au chocolat, wander round the local market, visit the *pharmacie* to stock up on one or two beauty products, browse old bookshops and just soak up French life and French manners, which I find rather charming. I want to believe that by surrounding myself in *Frenchness,* I can capture some of the magic and bring it back home with me. Being from and living in the UK, I'm already well-immersed in European lifestyle; the French, however, do seem to have a certain way of doing things that makes life just that bit sweeter and more refined and elegant. When I want to get that 'sweet French touch' back but can't just drop everything and jet off to France to do so, I get myself into 'French chic' mode and think back to how life was when I did live amongst the French in my younger days, reconnect with French friends, ponder on some of the little tips and tricks I picked up during my time there and bear in mind that I can bring French chic and the French way of life to me, wherever I am.

Please read on to discover some of the petite lessons I learnt whilst living in France; secrets of beauty, how French chic women stay slim, mystique, charm and how to live simply but well. For me, what French chic *isn't* is plumped-up lips, boob jobs, full makeup and hair, lots of flashy labels on show, talking loudly, getting drunk, stuffing yourself with takeaways and junk food, looking overdone or too put together and detailing your whole life on social media; it's a more natural and simple beauty and understated way of being such as taking good care of yourself, savouring 'real' rather than processed foods, subtle makeup, natural hair, being immaculately dressed yet still a little laid-back or *décontracté*, adhering to strict hygiene and skincare practices, wearing a signature scent, reading books, being more reserved, not caring too much what people think of you and taking the time to enjoy simple pleasures in life. I hope this little book and its petite lessons will sweeten your life and bring some French chic into your days, wherever you live in the world.

Eat & Drink à la Française

*"The worst disease is scorn of one's
own body." - Montaigne*

*"The most beautiful thing is the belief
that you are." - Unknown*

I Just love the above two quotes; particularly the second. One thing I really noticed whilst living among the French was a sense of high self-esteem and self-regard all around and this need to always present your best self. No slobbing around with old joggers on and slurping a giant soda for them. This feeling of worthiness didn't seem to just be reserved for sylphlike creatures and model-types but was something almost all of the French women I came across seemed to embrace. The French appear to have an innate sense that they are worth setting a table and making a nice meal for (even if they are only going to eat it on their own), worth the beauty creams they painstakingly select and use on a daily basis and worth, well, just caring for and looking after. Believing you are beautiful and taking the time to look after yourself are worthy pursuits in this modern age despite many believing they are old-fashioned concepts - your body is your permanent home during this lifetime, much more so than your physical address, and is worthy of a great deal more attention than that which many people lavish on their physical homes (and cars). Having a clean, comfortable and beautifully presented 'permanent home', or body, which you lovingly tend to and look after will impact greatly on your quality of life and enable you to live as healthy and abundant a life as possible.

Petite Lesson 1 – A nourishing diet is one of the best-kept French beauty secrets

Many women focus on using expensive creams and cosmetics or getting the latest professional treatments to improve their looks but pay little attention to what they're eating and drinking day to day. What they don't realise is that although some of these fancy creams, cosmetics and professional treatments will work to some extent, they won't do that much to improve overall beauty and appearance. A nutritious diet is an absolute essential if you want to look your beautiful best and will transform your skin, hair and figure a million times more than any cream, oil or treatment will. If you want to clear your skin, encourage more luxurious hair growth, look younger and more radiant and improve your happiness levels, please think about your diet.

French women tend to eat less, if any, processed and pre-packaged foods and prefer to eat 'real' foods which they prepare themselves. You don't need to be a great cook or spend a lot of time on this (unless you want to). A delicious, home-made soup can be rustled up in no time and accompanied with a little bread, salad and something protein-rich makes a super-quick and healthy, light dish and is a lot better for you than a ready-made meal. Beautiful skin, hair and nails start with nourishment from within and making sure you get all the nutrients you need is essential to looking good. Eating high-quality, whole foods is a huge factor when it comes to your appearance and a healthy diet will do more to make you attractive than any amount of expensive makeup or professional treatments will.

Petite Lesson 2 – French chic women control themselves around food

Not everyone is super-slim in France and around 50% of the French are in the slightly overweight to obese range, however the obesity problem which is engulfing many other countries just isn't as prevalent in France. Why is this? Aside from eating mainly whole and unprocessed foods, there are several other reasons but it has occurred to me that one may be because being overweight in France just isn't as accepted as it is in other countries. This may sound simplistic but there is definitely a social pressure to maintain your weight in France – not to be skinny but to be more or less the 'correct' weight for your height (according to government guidelines), give or take a few pounds. I believe that this 'pressure' to stay slim and the 'disapproval' which ensues if you do put on weight leads to French women being more motivated to exercise discipline and control around what they eat. Also, many French women just outright refuse to tolerate weight gain and are very careful to avoid this. If they do carry some extra pounds, they take sensible measures to remedy matters. French women know that balance is key and tend to nip any weight gain in the bud by making up for an evening of indulgence with lighter meals for a day or two to prevent things getting out of hand.

Portions in France are generally much smaller when eating out than in, say, the United States or the UK and the focus is on the quality of the food rather than quantity. The French take the time to sit down, savour and enjoy their meals and eat quite slowly compared to many other countries. Picking up food in a drive-thru and scoffing it on the go isn't really the done thing. A certain formality still prevails in French culture and food is generally eaten when seated and preferably with cutlery.

The French often eat their meals in courses, even if the starter is just a small soup and the dessert a slice of melon. Serving vegetables on the side in a separate dish is also quite usual; the trick is to serve each course or side dish on a small plate or bowl. Serving food in this way does make it seem like you're eating more than you actually are, therefore encouraging you to eat less, and also feels rather decadent.

Many French women seem to follow the 80/20 rule (even though they probably wouldn't refer to it as that) meaning they eat healthily around 80% of the time so that they can indulge in little treats the other 20%. Treats are always included, even when trying to lose weight; it's just done in a sensible fashion.

Although many French smoke and people often assume this is the reason French women stay so slim, there are also many French who do not smoke who are slim and, really, it's a whole combination of factors, including cultural, which help French women to stay trim.

Petite Lesson 3 – Avoid diet foods at all costs, whether or not you're trying to slim down

Diet foods really aren't a great option and won't fill you up for long. Diet and low-fat/no-fat foods are usually highly-processed foods which are low in calories but, because the fat has been removed, hidden sugars and other unhealthy ingredients are added to replace the fat which mount up the calories. These foods won't satiate you and may even lead to you feeling more hungry.

It has been proven that consuming the naturally-occurring fat in whole, natural, unprocessed foods in moderate amounts isn't harmful to your health and will fill you up – just keep an eye on your quantities.

I'm a big fan of that modern concept of only eating foods your grandparents would recognise - something the French (and many other nationalities) have been doing since forever without really considering it a 'thing'.

Petite Lesson 4 – How to lose weight the French chic way

Before moving to France when younger, I myself was a little plump and ate a very 'British diet' (which can be healthy, but not always!). Whilst living in France and mixing with the French, I picked up a whole new way of eating and viewing food and lost the weight I wanted to lose without too much thought other than just trying to fit in with my new French friends and emulate the locals.

My tips to lose weight the French chic way, which worked for me, are, firstly, to try to avoid the word *'diet'* and just focus on eating natural, unprocessed foods, *lots* of vegetables, treats in moderation and no snacking. This is common sense but sometimes it's so hard to do when you live in a country (such as the UK, where I live) where this style of eating is slowly being eroded. From my time spent living amongst the French, I observed that French women seemed very able to control themselves around food and not obsess about snacks and treats; I think this is because what they eat for their main meals is of *high quality* (not pre-prepared) and therefore nutritious and satisfying to the body and so they're not craving anything extra. The body craves food because it wants nourishment. It's better to eat 'real', whole foods (not processed and fat-free foods – good fats are good for you and will keep you feeling satiated; see more about this later). If you're trying to lose weight but aren't providing your body with the nutrients it requires whilst doing so, your self-control will waver and break down as your body quite rightly demands the food it needs to satisfy its daily nutrient requirements. So please don't punish your body – treat it well whatever its size and provide it with the nutrients it needs. Therefore, focus on eating *nutritious, unprocessed* foods so that your body gets the nourishment it needs on a daily basis to avoid creating nutritional gaps which can create cravings and the desire for snacks.

Focusing on eating unprocessed foods also means avoiding commercially-produced dressings and sauces, as far as you can, which often contain a lot of sugar. You could try using olive oil and/or balsamic vinegar and a squeeze of lemon as a dressing on salads and making your own sauces. It's best to also avoid things like sugary and diet yogurts and opt for the natural, full-fat, unsweetened version or a natural Greek-style yogurt instead which you can sweeten yourself with dried fruits or a little honey. I did see a lot of tins/cans/jars of beans and pulses being purchased fairly often in French supermarkets but not really many processed 'ready' meals which quite often form the basis of many people's diets here in the UK.

I did notice that bread was eaten every day although always in moderation and always a good-quality bread (usually freshly bought each day).

The French eat a lot of fresh fruit and vegetables on a daily basis and incorporating fruit and vegetables into every meal can often be the difference between being slim and being overweight. If you're trying to lose weight, adding a side dish of a cooked, chunky vegetable (eg carrots or similar, but preferably not potatoes which can be quite calorific) to your main meal can really help to fill you up.

Include a daily treat such as good-quality chocolate. The 'good-quality' part is important so please do try to get a taste for the more nutritious dark chocolate (if you don't already have a taste for it!). A chocolate with a minimum of 70% cacao is preferred; I often have a few squares of a good-quality 37% chocolate together with some squares of 85% - it makes for quite a delicious combination! Dark chocolate is considered rather nutrient-dense (it's high in magnesium amongst other things) and is therefore more satiating. You can also control yourself more when eating a good-quality chocolate rather than a cheaper, sugar-filled chocolate bar with little actual cacao in. Keep an eye on your quantities – a few squares a day should be enough to give you that chocolate fix. If I fancy a chocolate biscuit, I often just have a couple of wholemeal biscuits such as oatcakes (which are quite readily available here in the UK and I think more further afield now) and eat them with a square or two of dark chocolate to make my own 'healthy' version of chocolate biscuits. Being a Brit, I do like to nibble on a biscuit with my 'cuppa' now and then...

Have three meals a day – breakfast, lunch and dinner (but only if you're hungry). You can work out the timings according to what suits you best, for example if you're not hungry in the morning, don't force a breakfast down you – les *femmes françaises* do not eat if not hungry. One little trick I have learnt is to package my breakfast up along with a little spoon and take it to work with me if I'm not hungry or don't have the time to eat breakfast before leaving the house; that way I can have it later in the morning when I can truly appreciate and savour it.

Most people's diets, according to government guidelines, should be made up of roughly 45-65% carbohydrates, 10-35% protein and 20-35% fat each day (slightly less carbohydrate, around 10-30%, and slightly more protein, around 40-50%, and fat, around 30-40%, if you're trying to slim down). A high-protein diet not only helps you lose weight but will also help stabilise blood sugar levels. This may all sound a bit complicated but is actually quite simple and gives a good rough basis of what kinds of foods to focus on.

As above, make sure you eat enough protein and fat – this is key to ensuring you feel satiated – not stuffed but not hungry either. Good sources of protein include lean meats, fish, seafood, dairy, eggs, nuts, seeds, beans and pulses. Vegetarians and vegans should ensure they're eating enough protein each day. Protein makes up your organs, bones and hair and contributes greatly to 'good looks'. Good fat sources include good oils (such as olive oil), olives, fatty fish, eggs, avocado and nuts and seeds. Good fats are good for you and keep you feeling full so you will eat less overall (this is why 'fat-free' foods really aren't a good option). Avoid 'bad' fats which are found in most packaged foods and some margarines.

Most people have no problem getting enough carbohydrates in their diet; unfortunately, though, it's usually the unhealthy kind such as pastries, cakes, biscuits, cookies, sodas & other highly-processed foods which can contribute to things like weight gain, hormone imbalance and diabetes. Healthier sources of carbohydrates include small amounts of bread, pasta and potatoes and larger quantities of vegetables, fruits and beans. I am rather partial to a biscuit myself so try to avoid having them in the house...

Try eating from a smaller plate. Visually, it makes you believe you're eating more than you actually are and feels more delicate and dainty in the process!

French women eat less overall. When it comes to your main meal of the day, half your plate should really be vegetables. As mentioned previously, if you're very hungry, prepare some cooked, chunky vegetables such as carrots or whatever other chunky vegetable is in season (ideally not potatoes which can be quite high in calories) and serve on the side in a separate dish; this should help to fill you up.

If you must have dessert each day, you can – just make it a fairly healthy option such as fruit and yogurt or even a couple of wholemeal biscuits or oatcakes with a piece of cheese.

It's useful to know the calorie content of foods but please don't get obsessed. It's more *what* you eat that matters. Focus on embracing a more French chic way of eating by preparing real, non-processed foods at home and eating a lot more vegetables and you'll find you naturally lose weight without too much pain and suffering!

Petite Lesson 5 – Homecooking is a big thing in France

Homecooking is still the norm in France and possibly another reason as to why French women manage to stay slim. In countries where pre-prepared, convenience foods and takeaways are increasingly being consumed, people are getting fatter and more unhealthy. The French generally say *non* to pre-packaged meals that are heated in the oven or microwave and more often than not put together nourishing and tasty meals made from scratch with fresh ingredients. This doesn't have to be anything fancy and can just be a homemade soup with crusty bread, a piece of cheese and salad. Making your own (simple) food doesn't have to take any longer than the time taken to heat a pre-packaged meal in the oven or for your takeaway to be delivered and the benefits of looking and feeling better are surely worth it.

Takeaways, ready meals and constant eating out are, I believe, a huge factor when it comes to putting on weight; if people just did a little more cooking at home using fresh and natural, 'real' ingredients like they do in France, weight gain would be much less of an issue in society. It's hard to keep an eye on the calories and nutritional content of takeaway foods and more often than not they're just another form of junk food (along with 'diet' foods) and won't do your body or your looks any favours.

If you are invited round to a friend's house for a light bite in France, it would be most unusual to be given something shop-bought and pre-prepared (unless that something was a sweet treat from the local bakery). Ordering in just isn't the done thing. You would most likely be eating something prepared at home, even if that were just a simple affair like bread, cheese and cold meats or a little pasta dish and some wine to drink.

Petite Lesson 6 – Smaller portions & no doggy bags

When eating out in France, portion size is much smaller than in, say, the UK or United States. The food is generally also fresher and therefore more nutritious. The body does need time to adjust to eating a bit less; if you've been eating large amounts for a long time and are then faced with a smaller plate of food than you're used to, this can be rather a *shock* for the body. Eating slowly and eating until you're *almost* full is the best option so please practise moderation. Remember, too, that being hungry before your next meal isn't a bad thing…

And please, no doggy bags. This is such a 'foreign' concept to the French and is considered somewhat distasteful. I would even go so far as to say it is looked down upon. They wonder why you would want to be served a plate of food so large that you couldn't possibly eat it all and then stuff the remainder into a 'doggy bag' that you take home and eat cold for supper/breakfast. The French prefer to just enjoy the moment and the dining out experience and focus on the quality of the food rather than how much they're getting.

Petite Lesson 7 – Snacking is frowned upon

If you're eating three nourishing meals a day, you shouldn't really need to snack. The French don't often snack and if you were to have a wander round a French supermarket, you'd see their snack options are very limited and nothing like what you'd see in countries such as the UK and United States where snacking is big business! French women are quite disciplined when it comes to set mealtimes and, rather than snacking, will save themselves for their next delicious meal of the day. The trick is the three meals they're eating each day are providing a combination of fat, fibre and protein which keeps them feeling satisfied, so the need to reach for a snack is much less. Snacking in France is mainly for children after school.

There are many, what I refer to as 'cardboard-like', snacks which are heavily marketed in several countries – you'll know the kind of snacks I mean; low-calorie biscuit packs and even just ordinary biscuits, cereal bars, crackers, crisps (or chips, as they're known in the United States), this kind of thing, which don't fill you up very much and have hardly any nutrition. If you are very hungry between meals and *really* need a snack, do as French women do and try to make it protein-based as this will actually fill you up (whereas those 'cardboard-style' snacks will not). Good snack options include a piece of cheese (with a couple of wholemeal crackers if you fancy), a handful of nuts or some natural, unsweetened yogurt - you can sweeten this yourself with some dried fruits (raisins, dates or chopped figs etc) and/or berries. You could also add some stewed or baked fruit (eg apples) and a sprinkling of cinnamon to make a delicious and more decadent snack (or dessert). If you really want something sweet, have a few squares of dark chocolate (with a handful of nuts if you fancy, to add in a bit of protein). Or for a real sweet treat, break off a small chunk of baguette and have it with a few squares of dark chocolate to make your own homemade pain au chocolat. Try to serve your snack as you would a meal – with a plate/bowl and a little napkin and take the time to sit down for a few moments to eat your snack so that you can appreciate the flavours as well as digest it properly. How often do you see a French woman gulping something down while out on the go? It's just not done. Eating (and snacking) in France is carried out in a more civilized fashion. And please don't eat anything straight from a bag, *ever*!

As mentioned above, snacking in France really isn't a *thing* and is mainly reserved for children when they finish school, therefore if you're finding you're looking for a snack between meals on a daily basis, do take another look at what you're eating for each of your three meals a day and make some adjustments to ensure you're properly satiated after your meals. Remember, too, that a black coffee rather than a snack may be all you need to pep you up between meals, and that hunger for a short time before your next meal is perfectly natural and it's not a bad thing to let yourself feel *slightly* hungry before tucking into your next dish of the day. I say 'slightly' hungry as you don't want to be famished. If you are very hungry then please do take another look at what you're eating for each meal to ensure you're properly satiated at mealtimes.

More decadent treats such as a pain au chocolat, croissant or other delicacy or dessert from the bakery are definitely something French women enjoy and savour on a regular basis, but maybe just as a treat at the weekend, not every day.

Petite Lesson 8 – French chic women don't partake in le binge drinking

I've never actually seen a *'plastered'* drunk French woman (or man) whilst out and about in France despite seeing this kind of thing *often* in my native UK. This may be partly due to the fact that France remains a somewhat socially conservative country in some respects whereby it's rather frowned upon and seen as quite *unsophisticated* for a woman to be seen staggering around drunk whilst out in public. Some of my French friends have commented on the fact that they are appalled by the level of binge drinking in the UK. They just can't understand why people would want to drink themselves into oblivion on a Friday night and ruin the whole weekend. French women do enjoy alcohol, especially wine, but it's savoured in a small glass and in an elegant manner and isn't guzzled down in a massive goblet with the intention of getting *'hammered'*.

Despite the annual consumption of alcohol in France being slightly higher than in the UK, binge drinking is very rare and the alcohol consumed is usually with a meal or nibbles. The French just seem so much more civilized around alcohol and are more disciplined as regards the premature ageing and weight gain effects of alcohol; it's just not worth it to them. There are also lots of French women, including young women, who don't drink alcohol at all, or very rarely, maybe just on a special occasion such as a birthday. Alcohol is one of the biggest agers there is and cutting back on your alcohol consumption will definitely improve your looks, especially your skin and eyes (and possibly increase your hair thickness too) and can dramatically influence your weight. Alcohol contains *a lot* of calories and, if you currently drink a fair amount and try cutting back, it's highly likely you'll notice a difference as regards weight loss.

Petite Lesson 9 – Just say non to sodas

Regular sodas are full of sugar and sure to promote weight gain if you're not burning it off. Diet sodas really aren't much better and can still be associated with weight gain, despite the fact they have zero calories. This is due to the fact that when artificial sweeteners (like in diet sodas) hit your brain, your body produces insulin to process the anticipated sugar. When this sugar doesn't arrive, your body becomes confused and metabolic processes are disrupted. Diet soda is actually much sweeter than regular soda and is likely to leave you craving more sugar in the long run.

This goes for 'diet' foods sweetened with artificial sweetener also – these are usually much sweeter than non-diet foods and really not good for you or your waistline. Try to follow the French chic example and stick to water, unsweetened tea and coffee and the occasional wine/tipple.

Skin, Hair, Scent
& Parisian style

"Act like Audrey. Dress like Jackie." – Unknown

Both Audrey Hepburn and Jackie Kennedy Onassis (see quote above) were considered style icons of their time and women who emanated grace, poise and charm. Although not French, they did seem to embody the spirit of *French chic*. Hepburn's unconventional yet still very feminine beauty broke the mould and defied social norms of the time in that she represented a somewhat 'alternative femininity' and created her own look which was quite different from the fashionable 'femme fatale' style which predominated in American cinema at the time – she didn't possess the highly desired hourglass figure typified by popular movie stars such as the overtly glamorous Marilyn Monroe, but was very slender; she wore classic, understated clothes (including trousers which weren't that acceptable for women in the mid-1950s) rather than full-skirted dresses, corsets and girdles and sported a very 'natural' makeup with defined eyebrows as opposed to thick cream foundation and the fashionable 'mask effect' look of the 50s. She was and still is a role model for gracious living and was elegant yet humble, seemingly quite unaware of her beauty. She even made being considered introverted and introspective something of an asset! Maybe this is why I admire Audrey so much; I am definitely something of a homebody and an introvert myself. She once stated: "I'd be quite happy if I spent from Saturday night until Monday morning alone in my apartment. That's how I refuel." In this modern age of 'he who shouts loudest' and exhibitionism, I find that quite refreshing (and reassuring).

Jackie Kennedy Onassis is to this day considered a fashion icon and her minimal and sophisticated, young yet ladylike 'Jackie look' is still widely copied; A-line shift dresses, boxy jackets, white jeans, low heels, pearls and, especially, the oversized sunglasses. The former First Lady adored fashion and makeup and epitomised timeless elegance and classy behaviour. She also adored Paris and spent a year there as a 20-year old college student and spoke fluent French. It's been said that there was a lot more to her behind the glamorous exterior.

I am also something of a fan of the more contemporary (and French) style icon, Parisian actress Clémence Poésy, who comes across as very natural and understated, both in the way she dresses and does her hair, as well as her very subtle makeup, although apparently she won't be without fragrance; as well as the former French First Lady, Carla Bruni, who displays grace, fabulous style and a rather bohemian kind of charm.

All of the above women, for me, epitomise the French chic look and way of being; women who come across as happy in their own skin, flaws and all. The lessons I have learnt from these four women are to celebrate who you are, create your own look and just be yourself; no mean feat in a world which constantly puts pressure on women to look and act in a certain way.

Petite Lesson 10 – Get serious about skincare

Good skin is the result of good hygiene; cleansing your face well at night, staying away from heavy makeup that can clog pores, sleeping well and eating healthily. Beautiful skin is a real asset and many French women begin a skincare routine as young as 12 years old, even if it's just using a moisturising lotion. It's not uncommon for French mothers to take their children to a dermatologist during the early teenage years just so that they can learn the basics of skincare and how to deal with any skin concerns that might arise.

French women tend to put more effort into skincare than they do perfecting the latest makeup technique. The natural look is *de rigeur* in France and many French *femmes* prefer their glowing skin to be the focus rather than the makeup. When you look after your skin, you will look great with or without makeup. A certain discipline is required to care for your skin on a daily basis but if you make the cleansing process an enjoyable one with lovely products (these don't need to be expensive), it can be something you look forward to each day and can provide an element of comfort and stability to your day.

The first step to looking after your skin is to double cleanse each evening before bed. The double cleanse involves cleansing your face with two different types of cleanser, one right after the other. Or you can use the same cleanser twice. The purpose of the first cleanse is to remove any makeup and sunscreen on your skin and the second to ensure your cleanser reaches your actual skin once any makeup and creams have been removed by way of the first cleanse. I prefer to massage in a light cream cleanser for the first cleanse and wipe off with a cotton pad, ensuring all traces of makeup are removed, and then for the second cleanse I will use a water-based cleanser, such as a gentle foaming facial wash, as I prefer to rinse after my second cleanse to make sure all traces of both cleansers are thoroughly removed and there is nothing sitting on my skin that might clog my pores. There is no real need to double cleanse in the morning as all that's needed then is a light cleanse (I prefer a rinse-off wash) to gently clean the skin.

After cleansing comes using a toner although personally I prefer to skip that step and just splash my face with cold water after rinsing off my foaming cleanser. If you are using a rinse-off cleanser then a toner isn't an absolute necessity. Some modern toners, however, do impart great benefits and it's worth taking a look at what's available.

Eye cream and moisturiser come next and I've heard it said many times that if you want to invest in one area of your skincare routine, this would be it. French *pharmacies* are a great place to purchase quality moisturisers and eye creams and most of the big French pharmacy brands are now available worldwide.

Sunscreen is an essential step each morning after applying your moisturiser and is a big factor in preventing premature ageing so please don't scrimp on this step. If you're like me and find that some sunscreens block your pores and cause spots, find a lightweight, non pore-clogging sunscreen which is meant for spot-prone skin – I recently found a good one from one of the big French pharmacy lines. You can even use your sunscreen without moisturiser underneath (just your eye cream) during the hottest summer days to avoid smearing too much product onto your skin if you're prone to spots.

A weekly or twice-weekly exfoliation is essential to remove dead skin cells; the French tend to recommend a gentle exfoliator rather than a rough scrub which can cause small 'tears' in the skin. Some serums and toners, such as those containing glycolic acid, also have exfoliating properties and could be a great addition to your skincare routine – just make sure you follow the instructions. Masks are useful in treating specific skin complaints such as breakouts or dehydrated skin; shop around to find what suits you best or you could even make your own. I personally love a peel-off mask! French women do tend to use masks fairly often and consider this regular pampering an enjoyable activity and an opportunity to take a break rather than a chore. Remember that caring for your skin should be considered an act of kindness.

Petite Lesson 11 – When it comes to makeup, aim to look like everything is completely natural

French women tend to wear very little makeup and prefer to put their efforts into perfecting their skin rather than their makeup look.   It's not very usual to see a full face of makeup in France and often it's hard to tell if a French woman is even wearing any makeup (they usually are). To achieve the natural look, do as French women do and skip foundation and use just a little concealer and powder instead. If you *must* replace the foundation with something, try a tinted moisturiser or one of the more recent BB or CC creams; most have a great texture and look very natural. Personally, I prefer just concealer and a light powder as I still get the odd spot and don't like to clog my pores too much. Also, I find a good sunscreen can act almost like a 'primer', blurring any imperfections so that I don't need anything more than just concealer. I like a loose powder, again so that I'm not clogging my pores, but if you prefer a little more coverage, a light dusting of a pressed powder would be ideal. A touch of bronzer or blush, mascara and lipbalm, lip gloss or lipstick finishes off the French 'no-makeup' look perfectly.

Petite Lesson 12 – Don't mess with your hair too much (but do mess it up a little)

French hair is usually very natural. Keep it clean and conditioned, as close to your natural hair colour and texture as possible and don't wash it too much; once or twice a week is ideal. It's not uncommon in France for women to wash their hair just once a week. If you feel like you need to wash your hair more often than that, just ensure you use a mild shampoo. Look after your hair's condition by occasionally massaging through a pre-wash hair oil (like coconut oil) an hour or so before shampooing; this can be very helpful if you have thick, frizzy and dry hair and also helps aid hair growth. Deep-conditioning masks for use after shampooing are also great for improving the hair's condition. Try to keep any styling products to a minimum if you want the natural look. I like to just use a small amount of hair oil after shampooing and conditioning on wet hair and will sometimes add a touch more between washes if my ends look a little dry. Some of the

French women I know will semi-dry their hair with a hairdryer but many just wash their hair at night or on their day off and leave it to air dry. You can pin or clip it in a certain way while you're air drying to allow your hair to 'set' in a particular way if you prefer. French hair is usually ever so slightly 'messed-up' and they like the tousled, more natural look. If your hair is naturally curly, just embrace its natural wave – a little hair oil applied to still-damp hair after washing and conditioning is wonderful stuff for taming curls and frizz. Don't forget to have your hair trimmed regularly at the hairdresser; the French may go for the natural look but they do still take good care of their hair and like to have a good cut.

Remember that good nutrition will not only benefit your skin, but is also essential for strong and healthy hair. A lack of B vitamins, iron and other nutrients can have a profound effect on hair health so do ensure you're eating a good diet to help feed your hair follicles from within; eating nutritious food will do so much more for the condition and thickness of your hair than any amount of masks or oils will. In fact, I would even go so far as to recommend that you spend your money on good food rather than expensive hair products or treatments if you want thick, luxurious and healthy-looking hair.

Petite Lesson 13 – Perfume is not a frivolous extra, it's an essential

Most French chic women wear perfume and many wouldn't even consider leaving the house without spritzing on their signature scent (some may have a small selection of different scents for different occasions). Perfume is for both yourself and others, but do keep it subtle; you want your scent to be a pleasant experience for all involved! Perfume is usually spritzed onto the back of the neck area and wrists. Perfume can transport you mentally to another time and place, whether that's to somewhere in the past or to a future you have envisaged for yourself; just as armchair travel can allow you to experience the world without leaving home, perfume can similarly take you to faraway places. Our choice of perfume is a reminder of our vision of ourselves and the future we want to create.

It can be considered a little rude to ask a French woman what perfume she's wearing, mainly because scent is such a personal thing and the French chic *femme* wouldn't want that you rush out to buy the exact same fragrance; she wants that *that* particular perfume is unique only to her and that others associate it with her and her alone.

Petite Lesson 14 – Parisian style

Parisian style is a slightly more polished and elevated version of French style. The chic Parisian tends to follow the trends just a little more closely than those living elsewhere in France, however whilst she may update her wardrobe with one or two on-trend pieces each year, she won't go overboard and her overall look will continue to be that of understated, timeless pieces put together in a highly polished yet slightly 'undone' way; the Parisian *femme* doesn't like to look too dressed up or overdone. As Coco Chanel advised: "It is always better to be slightly underdressed". The Parisian look tends to be discreetly chic and more classic than daring, even a little 'safe'. The Parisian doesn't like to look like she's tried too hard but she will take the time to ensure her clothes are well-pressed, shoes polished, her handbag matches the outfit and any accessories are down to the *bare minimum.* The aim is to look well-groomed but in a natural and effortless way.

The chic Parisian will seek out a few high-end pieces that will last for *years.* Often she'll go high-end for outerwear, bags, shoes and accessories but high street for the rest (unless her budget is above average). Investing in a quality coat, a fabulous bag and good shoes and scarves means whatever else she's wearing is instantly upgraded and doesn't need to work quite so hard. This high-low mix is key to achieving Parisian chic. A selection of everyday basics which are reasonably priced and made in natural fabrics, combined with high-quality statement pieces, are all you need to create a Parisian chic capsule wardrobe. When your coat, shoes and/or bag are more high-end, the rest of your outfit will be elevated as a result.

"Simplicity, good taste and grooming are the three fundamentals of good dressing and these do not cost money." – Christian Dior

Petite Lesson 15 – Look more polished by spending less

There's no need for a major decluttering, but do take a good look at the clothes, shoes and accessories you currently own and get rid of anything you don't like or that doesn't fit properly. French chic women tend to have a lot less in their wardrobes because their motto is 'buy less, but better'. Think quality not quantity and refuse to buy cheap clothing in bulk that you end up having to replace year after year. Think long-lasting, timeless, quality items that'll last for years to come. When you stop frittering your money on countless cheap items that wear out quickly, you'll find you have the spare cash you need to invest in a few higher-quality items, plus money left over. This strategy is also very useful if you're something of a compulsive shopper like I used to be and can cure your shopping 'addiction' practically overnight. Taking your time and only purchasing something after much consideration, whether that's a high-end piece or a lower-priced basic, is the key to building a quality, Parisian-style capsule wardrobe.

Petite Lesson 16 – Mix casual and high-end

Focus on investing in high-end outerwear, bags, shoes and scarves which you can combine with more accessibly-priced basics from the high street. When purchasing higher-quality pieces, avoid any obvious logos; the aim is to look elegantly understated in a quietly expensive and not obvious way. Thinking about high-quality investment pieces, you only really need a good winter coat (in wool) and a quality trench, one fantastic handbag (for day), perhaps in a crossbody style, a couple of pairs of good shoes (maybe ankle boots and ballet flats/loafers) and one or two scarves; lightweight for spring and ideally cashmere for winter. I would also add a pair of quality oversized sunglasses to this list which, if you take care of them, should last for years. Acquiring a few key, high-end pieces which you pair with your more inexpensive, everyday basics will ensure you look chic and elegant but not too 'done'. The Parisian would never really wear an outfit comprised of only high-end pieces – this would just be too excessive and overly dressy.

Petite Lesson 17 – Curate a Parisian-style wardrobe

Fabric and fit are very important if you want to achieve the Parisian look. Try to stick to natural fabrics such as cotton, linen, wool, cashmere and silk which are better quality and will last longer, feel more comfortable and will allow your skin to breathe, especially in the warmer weather. Your clothes must fit properly if they are to look good so either try things on to make sure they fit well before purchasing or take them to a tailor to have them altered if the fit isn't quite right. Even though you may love an item and just *have* to have it, please don't even consider buying it if it doesn't sit well and you're not planning on taking it to a tailor straight away. Don't waste your money on items that don't fit; save your cash so that you can invest in a high-end piece that will upgrade and elevate your wardrobe so much more than a full-to-the-brim closet full of cheap and badly-fitting clothes will.

Parisian style is quite subdued and a natural, classic, even 'conservative' look is favoured. Parisians usually stick to neutral tones and tend to wear no more than two or three colours at a time (not including denim). They stick to shades such as black, grey, navy and white/beige/cream. And denim, of course. If wearing a print, they wouldn't wear more than one print in the same outfit. Parisians often inject some colour into their outfit with accessories, but even these are relatively understated.

Petite Lesson 18 – Aim to look impeccably 'dressed down'

Parisian style usually has an element of 'undone' about it; an effortless 'I don't care too much about my appearance' attitude where they never look like they're trying too hard or have spent hours getting ready. It's a 'done, but undone' style. This *nonchalance,* however, is a little deceiving and actually disguises the fact that Parisians spend quite a lot of time on the details of their outfit. The look is never too 'dressed up' or 'perfect' but it's never all-out casual either. It's a combination of quality basics put together with maybe one or two high-end pieces which automatically elevate the cheaper items. Parisians avoid anything too 'matchy', for example a matching bag and shoes, or matching earrings and necklace. Excellent attention to skincare and minimal makeup also serve to keep things as effortless and natural as possible. Parisians dress their best but there's nothing flashy about it; it's a tastefully alluring look but never overtly sexy and the goal is to look immaculate yet 'dressed down' at the same time.

Petite Lesson 19 – What to buy (les essentiels)

Here is a list of basics that many Parisian women have in their wardrobes – the list is not exhaustive but please select what appeals and aim to purchase your chosen items in natural fabrics such as cotton, wool, cashmere, linen or silk and ensure they fit well. Focus on spending a greater amount on high-quality outerwear such as coats or a smart jacket, accessories and shoes to elevate your more accessibly-priced, high street basics. Here is a list of what I consider to be *les essentiels:*

- Classic wool coat
- Lightweight trench
- Leather handbag
- Black jeans
- Dark blue jeans (not ripped)
- Silk camisole (in black or white/cream)
- Black dress
- Ankle-length, black, slim-fitting trousers
- Fine-knit polo or turtle neck
- Breton striped top
- Soft, silky blouse

- Close-fitting, lightweight puffer coat/jacket for winter
- Lightweight cotton/silk scarf & cashmere scarf
- Silky robe
- Ankle boots
- Ballet flats
- Pearl or sparkly stud earrings

Petite Lesson 20 – Wear your clothes well, whatever their cost (impeccable grooming)

Because Parisian women invest time, effort and money into curating a quality capsule wardrobe, they take good care of their clothes and accessories. Please look after your clothes and ensure you follow the washing instructions, repair as necessary, polish your shoes and protect your new leather handbag with a leather protector. Ensure your jewellery is clean and sparkling and regularly wipe your spectacles/sunglasses; I can't tell you the number of times I've come across somebody who was very well turned-out but with filthy glasses!

Excellent personal hygiene and good-quality, clean, well-pressed clothing put together in a chic and understated way will ensure you look impeccable, whatever the cost of your outfit.

Petite Lesson 21 – Shoes, accessories and lingerie

I saw a lot more lower-heeled and flat shoes being worn during my time in Paris and in other parts of France than anything with a very high heel or stilettos. Low-heeled or flat ankle and knee-high boots, ballet flats, loafers and lowish-heeled espadrilles in summer were most popular. Parisian and French fashion is quite subdued and laid-back and nothing says you're trying hard more than high heels. I did see high heels worn for more special occasions, just not as an everyday or work shoe. Whatever type of shoe you're wearing and whatever the cost, please ensure they are comfortable and fit well and are clean, polished and in good condition. Stick to neutral tones when purchasing shoes – blacks, browns and beiges are best – and try to make sure your shoes/boots will go well with what's in your wardrobe. I've heard it said a few times now that French and Parisian women rarely wear sports shoes or trainers but I definitely saw quite a lot of this type of shoe although it was usually a more delicate sports shoe or trainer. What I did notice was that sporty footwear was worn only with chic, fitted items and rarely with sports clothes or loose, baggy trousers/joggers/a hoodie; I saw sports shoes put together with ankle-length, slim-fitting jeans or trousers, with dresses, with beautiful coats (including trench coats) and/or with gorgeous handbags. The casualness of the sports shoes/trainers was balanced out by the sophistication of the rest of the outfit so that the overall look was quietly casual rather than 'in-your-face' sporty.

Aim to purchase one or two fairly good-quality scarves – if you love a bit of colour, you could buy these in brighter shades. It is customary for the Parisian to own a few scarves and to wear them regularly – maybe a nice silk scarf for when you want to look more dressy and a pashmina-style scarf for everyday or when it's a bit chilly out.

When it comes to jewellery, less is definitely more. A nice pair of pearl or sparkly stud earrings and a longer, more dangly pair for special occasions are all you really need. Wearing matching jewellery sets is a no-no and a bit over the top and too put together by Parisian standards. Maybe wear a necklace if you're not wearing earrings, or just a simple bracelet with very simple earrings; never all three. Rings are minimal. And please keep your jewellery clean!

Parisians like to invest in quality lingerie in order to provide a good foundation for their clothes. This doesn't need to be expensive but does need to be of a decent standard if it is to provide adequate support. I personally prefer cotton or lace over cotton, and for bras to be underwired which I feel offer more support. Comfort is everything so choose wisely.

Say *oui* to investing in a silky robe for those mornings/evenings when you want to lounge rather than slob at home and feel very French and *glamorous.*

How to be Charming & Lovely like a French Femme

"Whoever does not visit Paris regularly will never really be elegant." – Honoré de Balzac

If you need a touch of French chic inspiration, watch a French film or two (or embark on a little trip to France if you can) and let the *Frenchness* just wash over you. Soak it up; the melodic language, the beautiful scenery, the impeccable grooming, the mannerisms, the clothes and the little silk scarves. Observe how they dress, where they live and what and how they eat. Let yourself be *influenced* by all that's wonderful about French culture and decide for yourself what elements you would like to incorporate into your own life in order to be transformed into a more charming and lovely version of *you*.

Petite Lesson 22 –
Live a romantic life

The French love a little romance. Why not choose to live a life of romance whether or not you're coupled up? Many people are in relationships with little romance and yet there are others without a partner whose lives are filled with romance. Romance yourself! Fall in love with yourself and surround yourself with beauty and positivity. Pamper yourself by looking after yourself and eating well; cook a simple but delicious meal; take bubble baths; be more childlike and just *enjoy* the little things in life; buy some gorgeous-scented flowers for your home; dress up (in an effortlessly chic way *naturellement*), pop into town to visit a department store and sample some perfumes; find a lovely café to sit and gaze out the window in; visit your local library or second-hand bookshop and browse the books; get engrossed in a good book; watch a French or set-in-France film; buy a French magazine (even if you can't speak French) just to flick through and see how the French live; indulge in a delicious treat or a baguette from your local bakery; pretend you're *une femme française*, get your trench coat on and take a stroll in the rain (with your umbrella); take the time to seek out a trench coat if you don't already have one; always look for the beautiful in life and refuse to dwell on the negative. Fill yourself up with joyful thoughts so that you light yourself up from the inside out.

Petite Lesson 23 – Live in the 'être' ('to be')

The French are a little more relaxed when it comes to achieving and goal-setting and don't seem to feel this constant need to 'be the best they can be' and are often quite happy to just let things develop as they will and appreciate what they have rather than constantly chasing the next best thing. In other words, they seem happier to just *be.* They take the time to appreciate the little things in life such as the smell of freshly-baked bread, sunshine, cosy comfort indoors when it's raining outside, enjoying a leisurely lunch break, taking the time to prepare a simple homemade meal, devoting time each day to their skincare routine and don't think there's anything wrong with 'disappearing' (switching off their phones and being non-contactable) for a couple of hours to wander through a park or read a book if they feel it necessary. None of these things are seen as wasting time but are viewed as worthy pursuits in themselves and part of the joy of living, or *joie de vivre*, and delight in being alive. Most of us have a lot to be grateful for and quite often only notice all we have when we are deprived of something that we had previously taken for granted. Enjoy indulging in the little things in life and know that life can be beautiful even when it's not perfect.

Petite Lesson 24 – Beautiful posture and poise

Beautiful posture and poise are important elements of your presentation and the French seem to be very aware of this. Many are taught from a young age to 'stand up straight' and 'don't slouch' and they carry this with them into adulthood. To improve your posture, keep your shoulders back, your chin level with the floor and avoid slouching. Try to practise some core exercises to keep your abdominal muscles strong and keep up your perfect posture both at home and when out and about in order to train your muscles so that good posture starts to feel natural to you; this is as it should be.

Poise is defined in the dictionary as 'graceful and elegant bearing; balance; control'. I see poise as having the ability to maintain a certain composure if somebody offends or insults you and not reacting but keeping your cool and responding in your usual polite manner. Poise could also be described as having soft movements, light steps, gentle language and not being coarse or aggressive. No cursing or yelling! It's being a more gentle and delicate person;

tender and perceptive and aware of others' feelings. It's practising good manners and being kind; in some ways good manners are really just another form of kindness. It's not hurrying and rushing others. Slow down! *Calmez-vous!*

Petite Lesson 25 – Embrace your femininity

A lot of women nowadays seem to think it's somewhat shameful to be a 'feminine' woman and view things like taking the time to care for your skin or applying makeup as frivolous and even demeaning and associate the whole 'femininity' concept with downtrodden housewives of yesteryear or modern 'bimbos'. It *is* possible to be both strong and independent as well as a 'feminine' and 'soft' woman and being feminine should not be considered a flaw. Why not enjoy and embrace that complex mix of passion and sensibility which is what femininity is? To get in touch with your feminine side, be more soft and gentle. Stop rushing and crashing around and just slow down, take lighter steps when you walk, maintain a good posture, indulge in self-care, never be mean but always kind and gracious to others, convey warmth in your actions, don't be afraid to be sensitive and feel your feelings, listen to your heart and try to live your life accordingly, cherish your beauty, don't talk over others, be less controlling and just accept things as they are, accept help when offered, take the time to connect with nature and all the seasons (even the rain!), laugh often, be more childlike and playful and exude a girly charm, have good manners and be polite and charming at all times. Revel in your femininity!

Petite Lesson 26 – Take
a mini-vacation every day

Take the time to slow down and do nothing on a regular basis. Be a 'loafer' (or 'flâneur' in French) and take a trip to a part of town you don't know very well and just wander the streets taking in all you see. You might come across a little café you fancy stopping off at or a gorgeous boutique. Stop rushing and don't overbook yourself, particularly on your days off. Why not have a day just to yourself if you can? Try to organise yourself more so you can avoid any last-minute stress while getting ready for work or at any other time of day. Have a French day – read a French magazine, visit a French bakery if there's one in your town, watch a French film. Take time out from your daily life to go 'off grid' and 'disappear' – pop your phone into your handbag on silent and take yourself off to a little café/library/garden/park/somewhere peaceful at home to read a book, savour a little dark chocolate or just people watch – this will allow you to properly relax and give your brain a well-deserved break. Loafing and mooching around should be part of your daily routine, even if just for a half hour a day (ideally much more).

As Victor de Hugo stated, "To err is human. To loaf is Parisian."

Petite Lesson 27 –
Be more reserved

As the saying goes, "Pour vivre heureux, restons cachés" (in English, "To live happily, live hidden"). It's no secret that French women can come across as slightly aloof and rather private. This, I'm told, is just the French manner and the intention isn't to be unfriendly or unwelcoming; in fact, it's considered very respectful to keep a distance and allow people their personal space and is perceived as rather invasive, vulgar even, to ask somebody too many personal questions (despite this being seen as a sign of openness and friendliness in some other cultures). The French value discretion. Questions are acceptable, but French *femmes* would rather you asked them to recommend a nice café or where to acquire a decent trench than anything too *(quelle horreur!) personal!* Crossing the boundaries of personal intimacy is much frowned upon. The topic of money, earnings and personal wealth is a big no-no, as are overt displays of wealth. Even questions about your line of work can be considered intrusive. It's very rare for the French *femme* to reveal all, except to those very close to her, but even then she'll sometimes keep her cards close to herself. Too much self-promotion and talking about one's goals are also a big no-no and they see it as more elegant to be more discreet about one's achievements and goals. Bragging about your accomplishments is considered very rude and it's more French to let others discover how amazing you are in a less obvious way.

I remember once travelling by car with a friend back up to France from Spain and recall the very noticeable difference in volume levels on popping into a couple of café bars and a restaurant en route once across the French border. Compared to Spain, everything was so *quiet*! The French are really quite discreet when out and about and don't enjoy attracting too much attention. Not that the Spanish enjoy attracting lots of attention, but I had forgotten just how *private* the French were when out in public. Part of this is manners as the French value behaving appropriately and it is just not considered polite to speak loudly when out in a café or restaurant. They are very respectful towards others and are careful to speak in quieter tones when in public so as not to force those around them to listen in on their conversation. Avoid shouting in public, and no swearing (if you want to be considered *charming*). French women may occasionally get *furious*, as we all do, but somehow they usually manage to contain this and avoid any public dramas as it is just not *de rigeur* in French society to partake in such behaviour and is much frowned upon. They tend to resolve their problems in private and away from prying eyes. Exuding a cool and calm manner and refraining from public dramatics or getting overly excited and enthusiastic about things is considered a much more dignified way of behaving. Over-excitable *foreigners* are often not very well-tolerated – that sparky bounce, so often revered in other cultures, just isn't appreciated as much in France and can come across as self-importance or arrogance and is the opposite of the typically modest and somewhat demure behaviour displayed by many French people. A little reticence counts for so much more in France. As Coco Chanel stated: "Adornment, what a science! Beauty, what a weapon! Modesty, what elegance!".

Petite Lesson 28 – French mystique

French mystique describes that air of mystery, glamour and even secrecy that surrounds the French *femme*. It's a charismatic and very feminine allure that is hard to put your finger on. The aura of quiet confidence exuded by the often mysterious French *femme* inspires intrigue and makes you wonder what is her secret? Much of it is down to the fact that, as mentioned previously, the French value discretion and really don't like to reveal a lot about themselves and let the world see too much of them. They prefer to hold some things back and keep certain things private to maintain a certain distance. Take a tip from the French and be more private; people don't need to know everything about you and, although it's healthy to discuss problems at times, oversharing is a big no-no in France and, from my own personal experience, can sometimes cause you even more problems further down the line...

Avoid talking about others in a negative way. Speak more softly and don't talk over others, taking over a conversation; this can be quite boring for the other person and there's nothing mysterious about wittering on non-stop about nothing in particular. *Never* put yourself down in any way – to have an air of mystique you need to develop a quiet and self-assured confidence and trust and approve of yourself more rather than making decisions based on the opinions of others. Find your own style and don't follow the crowd too much. Think of some famous women you admire, French or not, and ask yourself how they practise the art of mystique. There is nothing loud or brash or overbearing when it comes to mystique; think quiet, even a little shy, laid-back, not revealing all, someone who doesn't blindly follow others just to fit in but is comfortable to do their own thing and pursue their own interests.

For me, the opposite of mystique would be to wear very revealing clothes, speak loudly, talk a lot about yourself and divulge many things which others may consider rather 'personal', seek others' approval before just going ahead and doing your own thing, bare all on social media, follow the crowd, be too afraid to say 'no' to invitations you really don't want to accept, get too comfortable and 'let yourself go' in a relationship, insisting on doing everything together and not pursuing your own hobbies, rush around and get in a tizz about trivial things and laugh too much and inappropriately; sometimes matters in life are serious and must be regarded as such. Incessant smiling and laughing in France are seen as superficial and not very sincere; the French tend to reserve their smiles and laughs for when they have real meaning.

You don't need to be classically beautiful to have mystique – often people are just drawn to others because there's 'something about them', a certain *je nais sais quoi.* French women know this and are happy to just make the most of who they are and embrace their flaws.

Try not to be too available and, more than anything else, *never* look as if you're trying too hard. Don't be afraid to say *non* to things you don't want to do; the art of saying *non* is very French and allows you to set healthy boundaries in your life and use your free time in a way that *you* want to. In this way, it is an act of self care. When somebody asks you for a favour or to attend an event, take a moment before replying rather than responding with an automatic 'yes'. Take the time to think and get back to the person later if need be; you could say something like: 'Thanks so much for asking but I think I might be busy that day, can I get back to you?'.

> *"In order to be irreplaceable, one must always be different"* – Coco Chanel

Petite Lesson 29 – Elegance

Elegance is defined as 'the quality of being graceful and stylish in appearance or manner'. You don't need to be dressed up to the nines with a fancy handbag to be elegant but you must get the basics right and be clean and presentable with good posture, neat and well-pressed clothes and have a gentle manner. Elegance is looking like yourself, accepting your flaws and not trying to change yourself too much. Showing too much skin is definitely not elegant, as is losing your temper and shouting at a waiter or sales assistant. Elegance is quality and simplicity. It's appreciating and being grateful for what you have and taking care of it. Coco Chanel said: "Elegance is refusal". For me, this means refusing to follow every latest trend and, in more general life terms, refusing to fall victim 'to the times' and go along with things just to fit in even when these things aren't really *you.*

Elegance isn't just about the way you dress, it's a way of life. You can dress as chicly and elegantly as you like but if you have an aggressive and rude manner, you will never be truly elegant. Beautiful posture, good manners and a kind nature are the cornerstones of elegance.

Avoid contributing to the swirls of gossip so prevalent in these modern times – being considered a little 'aloof' has to be better than being regarded as a whispering tittle-tattle and somebody who can't be trusted to keep information to herself. Remember that when you treat others with kindness, you automatically become more beautiful.

"Elegance is when the inside is as beautiful as the outside." – Coco Chanel

Petite Lesson 30 – Educate yourself

The French detest overt displays of wealth and would much rather look down their nose at you not because of your lack of earning power but, rather, based on the books you've read (or not read!). So take the time to be well-read; join your local library or visit some nearby thrift stores and browse their book selection. Or buy a few books from Amazon! Read book reviews online and note down those that take your fancy. Buy a newspaper that appeals and take an interest in the world. Newspapers can be a little negative at times but you will also find a lot of uplifting and interesting articles therein. Watch documentaries that pique your interest on television. Watch French films. Learn a language (French?). Be interested in others. Intellect is highly valued in France and considered quite an attractive quality, both in men and women. The French still buy newspapers regularly, read books and have conversations with others about what they're currently reading and what's going on in the world.

Petite Lesson 31 – How to get that insouciant French charm

The French tend to have a reputation for being somewhat *nonchalant*. In the English dictionary, 'nonchalant' is described as 'unconcerned, casually calm and relaxed, not displaying anxiety/interest'. It's true that the French do seem less concerned about what others think of them and are quite comfortable to tell you *non* if they don't want to do something. They don't seem to have that, to them very *foreign*, 'you must be the best at what you do' mentality and are a little more laid-back when setting goals (or, at least, they *pretend* to be, perhaps out of a fear of looking as if they're trying too hard!). And they certainly wouldn't dream of boasting about their accomplishments as this is seen as really quite *vulgar*. They have their goals and ambitions, of course, but appear much more relaxed and *laissez-faire* about the outcomes and are inclined to believe 'what will be will be'. The French can be rather practical in nature and know that worrying about the inane in life really won't affect the outcome and the best anyone can do is just accept their current situation and do the best they can within their capabilities and means to improve their circumstances and then just relax and know it's all being dealt with. They tend not to have their whole lives mapped out in advance and therefore can come across as slightly bohemian and free-spirited and seem happier to just accept where they are in life and take a day at a time in the pursuit of their goals.

If this way of life appeals, try to be more French and loosen up; it's important to have goals and ambitions and know the general direction in which you want your life to take but try to just enjoy the ride. Enjoy daily simple pleasures on the journey towards your goals and be open to the possibility that the goal you have in mind for yourself may not be what you end up with; life can often surprise you with something even better. Take on a more carefree outlook, do your best and just see what comes without forcing things. Be less 'uptight', mess up your hair a little and don't look too perfect when you head out the door. Don't reveal your insecurities and angst to all and sundry; do as the French do and discuss these things in private with people who have your best interests at heart. *Never* put yourself down in front of others; this is absolute anathema to the sophisticated French woman. Be independent and don't lose yourself in relationships or be too clingy – keep up your own interests and make sure you spend time apart doing your own thing from time to time. Learn to love yourself and don't rely on others for your self-esteem; focus on building yourself up from the inside out. How you view yourself and the world is up to you and you can make your thoughts as wonderful or as worrisome as you wish. Worry less and try not to pay attention to what people think of you. As Coco Chanel stated: "I don't care what you think of me. I don't think of you at all." Remember, too, that worrying less will benefit you in terms of fewer wrinkles and frown lines and who doesn't want that?

Petite French Chic Observations *(just for fun)*

- Spending all day trawling the shops for a simple €10 white T-shirt.
- Using a bargain basement shampoo but carefully applying a *trés* expensive face powder.
- Throwing on your old and battered denim jacket day in, day out but painstakingly buffing up your treasured leather ankle boots after every outing.
- Washing your face with soap and water but using an *amazing* moisturiser.
- Donning your silky robe to make any *difficult* phone calls.
- Being a little rude with a shop assistant who couldn't find your size but then feeling bad

and making up for it by taking mental note of her name and writing a fabulous online review later.

- Not buying any new clothing items in a whole year (because you don't need any).
- Wearing navy with black.
- Wearing a lot of black but breaking it up with a colourful accessory.
- Not running up debt on a credit card and buying only what you can afford.
- Spending two years trawling online shopping websites, flipping through magazines and making little excursions to out-of-the-way boutiques in distant parts of the city to *eventually* find the perfect classic winter coat.
- Religiously buying a newspaper every day but reading only the fashion pages.
- Looking down your nose at the people queuing in the fast food restaurant.
- Spending all weekend locked in your flat reading a book and not telling anyone where you are (only popping out for fresh bread and a *croissant*).
- Wishing for rain in summer and sun in winter.
- Donning your chic winter boots and glamorous fur-collar coat on the first official day of autumn, even though it's 22° outside.
- Travelling all the way across town to pick

up a delicious dessert from that *delightful* little bakery.

- Framing a magazine cover that you just *adore* and hanging it in your bedroom.
- Soaking up the sun on a hot summer's day despite meticulously applying factor 50 to your face all year round, including in winter. Who can resist catching a few rays of sun? One of the little pleasures in life...

Note from the Author

Thank you for purchasing this book. If you enjoyed it, please would you be kind enough to leave a review on Amazon? It'd be much appreciated!

Thank you, Caroline x

carolinedionauthor@outlook.com

Printed in Great Britain
by Amazon